SUNSHINE
MAKES THE
SEASONS

By Franklyn M. Branley

Illustrated By Shelley Freshman

SUNSHINE MAKES THE SEASONS

Thomas Y. Crowell Company · New York

LET'S-READ-AND-FIND-OUT SCIENCE BOOKS

Editors: *DR. ROMA GANS*, Professor Emeritus of Childhood Education, Teachers College, Columbia University
DR. FRANKLYN M. BRANLEY, Astronomer Emeritus and former Chairman of The American Museum-Hayden Planetarium

Library of Congress Cataloging in Publication Data Branley, Franklyn Mansfield, 1915- Sunshine makes the seasons. (Let's-read-and-find-out science book) SUMMARY: Describes how sunshine and the tilt of the earth's axis are responsible for the changing seasons. 1. Seasons—Juvenile literature.   [1. Seasons]   I. Freshman, Shelley, illus.   II. Title. QB631.B73   1974   525'.5   73-19694 ISBN 0-690-00437-0   ISBN 0-690-00438-9 (lib. bdg.)

2   3   4   5   6   7   8   9   10

SUNSHINE MAKES THE SEASONS

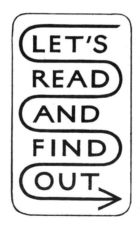

SUMMER
FALL
WINTER
SPRING

Seasons change as a year goes by. They change all over the world.

Not all parts of the world have the same season at the same time. It depends where you are. About December 21 winter begins in the northern part of the earth. But this is when summer begins in the southern part of the earth. When it's winter in Europe, Asia, and North America, it's summer in Australia, Africa, and South America.

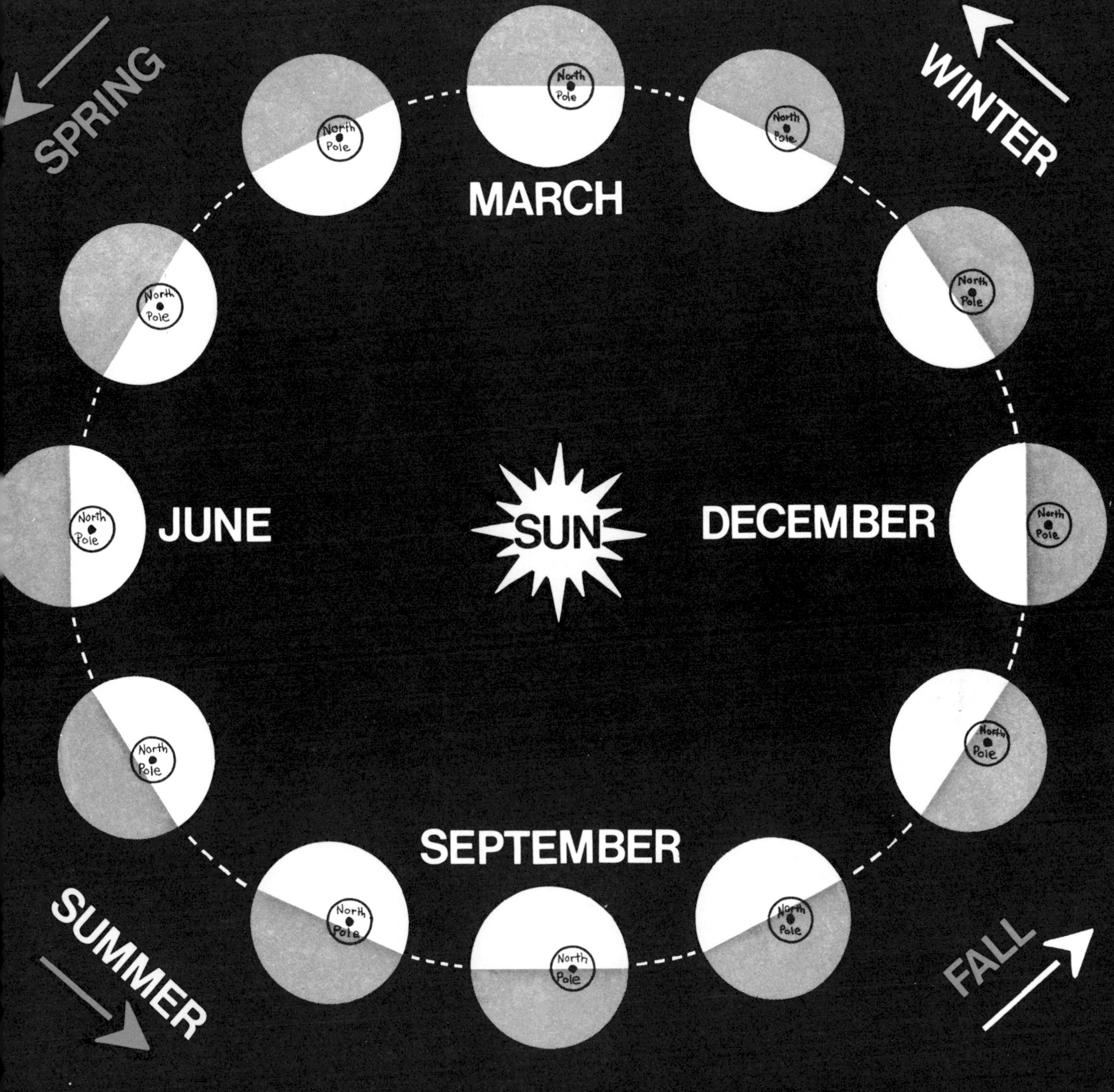

SPRING

WINTER

MARCH

JUNE

SUN

DECEMBER

SEPTEMBER

SUMMER

FALL

North Pole

1

The far northern part of the earth is the region of the North Pole. The far south is the region of the South Pole. Seasons change in the polar regions also. Winters are very cold. Summers are a bit warmer, but they are still cold. It never gets warm at the poles of the earth.

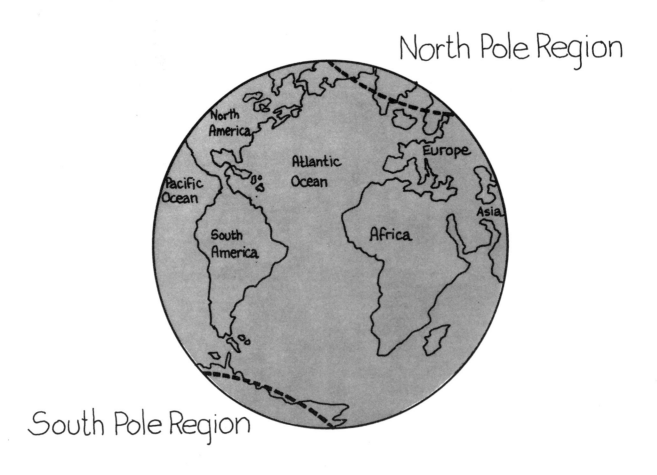

North Pole Region

South Pole Region

Summer at the North Pole.

3

Seasons change at the middle part of the earth, too—near the equator. Summers there are very warm. Winters are also warm, but not as warm as summer.

Winter at the equator.

5

It never gets cold at the equator, except on the very high mountains. It's always cold high on a mountain, even near the equator. It may be cold enough for snow to stay there all through the year.

Earth is a cold planet. If the sun did not shine, earth would never get warm. The heat of the earth comes from the sun.

The sun warms the earth. Air that surrounds the earth holds the heat. High on a mountain there is not much air. There's not enough to hold heat. That's why it's cold on a mountaintop.

VERY VERY THIN AIR

LESS AIR

NOT MUCH AIR

A LOT OF AIR

The sun warms the earth.
The air holds the heat.
Sunshine makes the seasons.

Earth is a big round ball. One half of the earth-ball is in sunshine. It's daylight on that half. The other half is in darkness. On that half it is night.

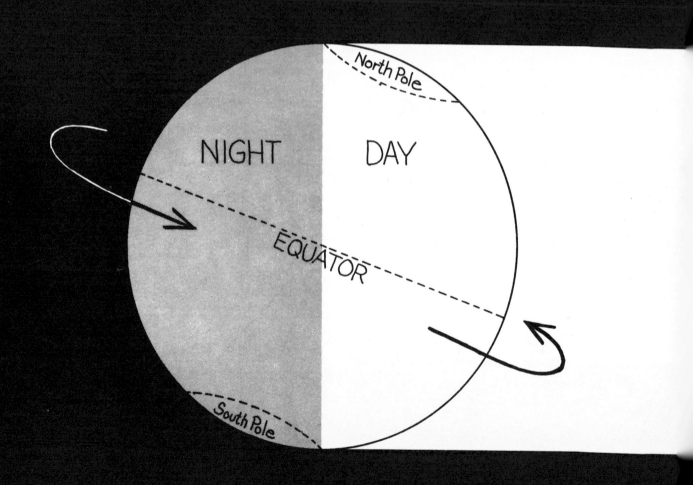

North Pole

NIGHT DAY

EQUATOR

South Pole

Because the earth spins, a place has daylight
and then darkness. Later it has daylight again. Do
you have daylight right now, or is it nighttime?
How long will it be before you have daylight, or
darkness?

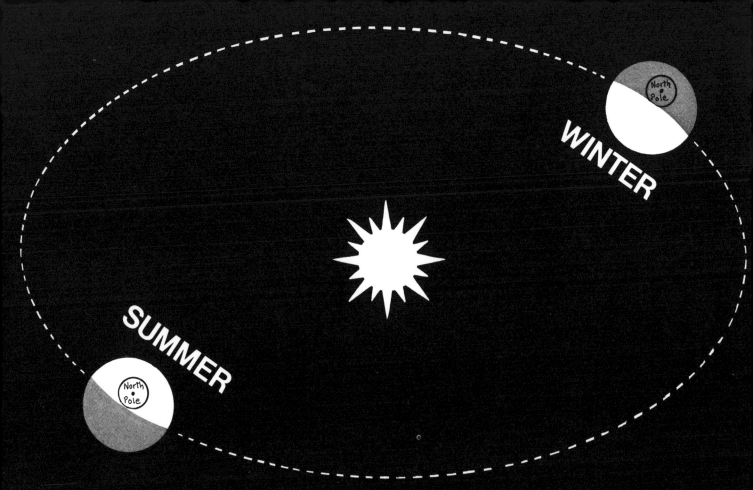

The length of daylight changes from season to season. In summer there's more daylight than in winter. In summer, nights are short. In winter, they are long. At the poles they are very long. A person at the North Pole or the South Pole would have daylight for six months. Then he would have six months of night.

Let's see why.

Suppose earth is a ball with a stick through it. The poles of the earth are where the stick comes through. The stick could be called the axis of the earth. Earth spins around its axis, just as the ball spins around the stick. There really is no stick through the earth. But earth spins as though there were one.

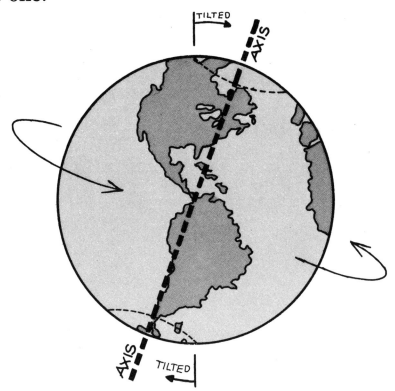

The axis of the earth is not straight up and down, though. The axis is tilted a little bit from the straight-up-and-down position. The tilt of earth's axis, and sunshine, make the seasons.

In July the northern part of the earth is tilted
toward the sun. That part of the earth has
summer. Half of the earth is in sunshine. It has
daylight. Half of the earth is in darkness. It has
night. Can you find where you live? Is it in
daylight? Later on you are carried into the dark
part of the earth and you have night.

Look at the North Pole. When you have daylight, it has daylight. But when you have night, the North Pole still has daylight. In summer the North Pole has daylight all the time.

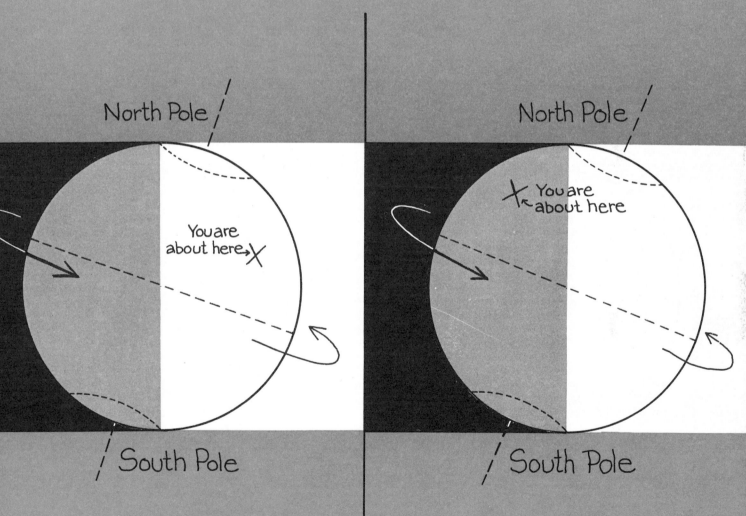

Six months later, it is winter in the north part of the earth. Find where you live. Suppose you are in daylight. Later on the spinning earth will carry you into darkness. But look at the North Pole. In winter the North Pole is in darkness all the time.

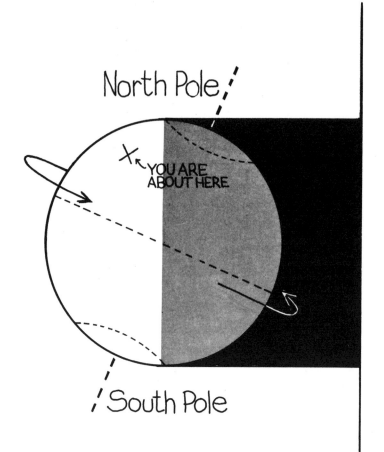

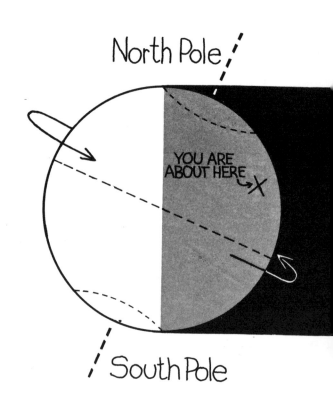

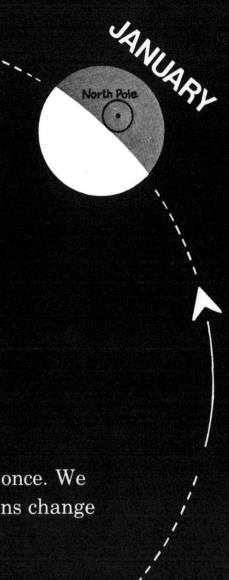

North Pole

In one year earth goes around the sun once. We say earth revolves around the sun. Seasons change as earth revolves around the sun.

In July the northern part of the earth gets a lot of sunshine, more than it gets in winter. It is summer and you can go fishing. You can swim in a pond or at the seashore. Bees are busy making honey. The weather is warm and it makes you feel lazy.

Days are long and nights are short. In summer it may still be daylight when you go to bed.

Near the North Pole it's even daylight at midnight. The sun shines so brightly at midnight that people have to wear sunglasses. They need dark shades on their windows so they can go to sleep. Places near the North Pole are called "lands of the midnight sun."

In July the southern part of the earth has winter. The South Pole is tilted away from the sun. It is dark there.

Six months after July it's January. Earth has moved halfway around the sun. The northern part is now tilted away from the sun. It is winter. If it's cold enough you can go ice skating. And if there's enough snow you can build a snowman, or go sleigh riding. Where the snow is deep, animals have a hard time finding food.

In winter days are short and nights are long. In winter it's dark when you go to bed and it's still dark when you get up—unless you sleep really late.

In winter the sun doesn't rise at the North Pole.
It is dark at bedtime. It is dark in the morning.
It's even dark at lunchtime. If people lived there,
lights would be turned on all through the day.

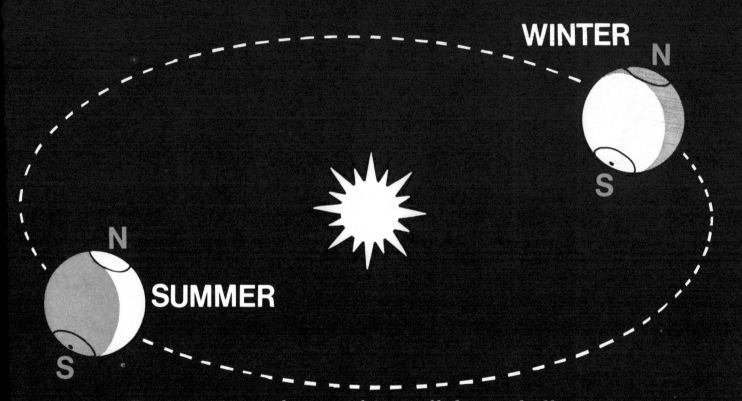

During winter the sun shines all day and all
night at the South Pole. That's because the South
Pole is tilted toward the sun.

In winter it's dark at the North Pole and light
at the South Pole. Sunshine makes the difference.

SPRING

North Pole

North Pole

FALL

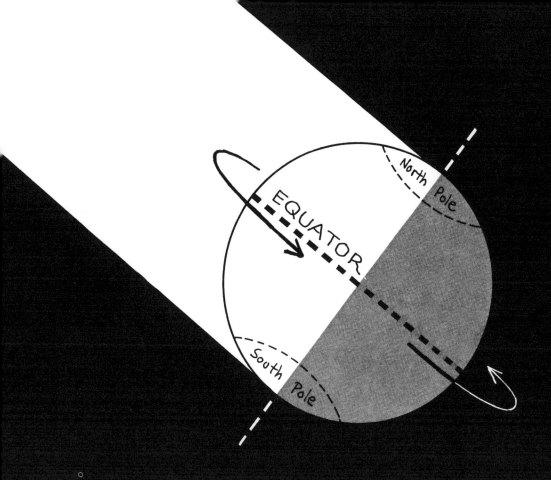

In spring and fall no part of the earth is tilted toward the sun. The sun shines right on the equator—halfway between the North Pole and the South Pole. All parts of the earth get just about the same number of hours of daylight and darkness.

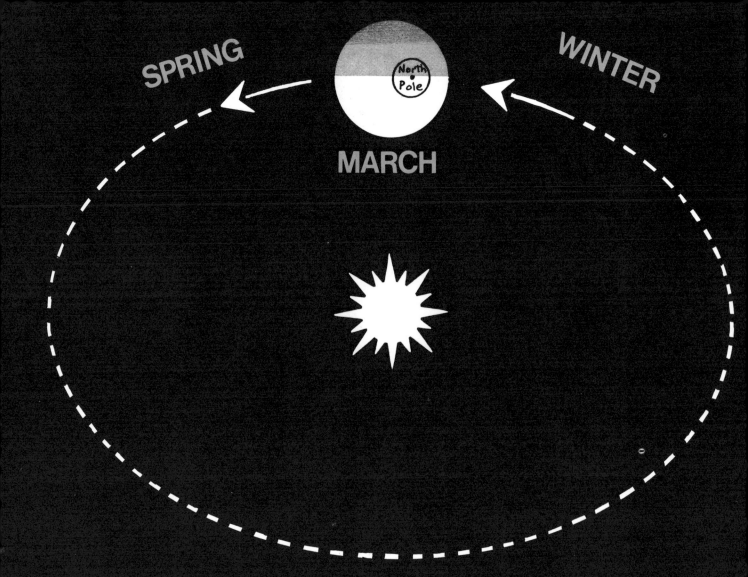

SPRING

WINTER

MARCH

Spring is the season that begins at the end of winter. It lasts about three months. It is the season when daffodils bloom. Birds build their nests. Apple trees are in blossom.

Spring is when grass, bushes, and trees turn green. What do you do in the springtime?

25

Fall, or autumn, is the season between summer and winter. In the northern part of the earth the weather gets cooler. Leaves on oak and maple trees change color and fall to the ground.

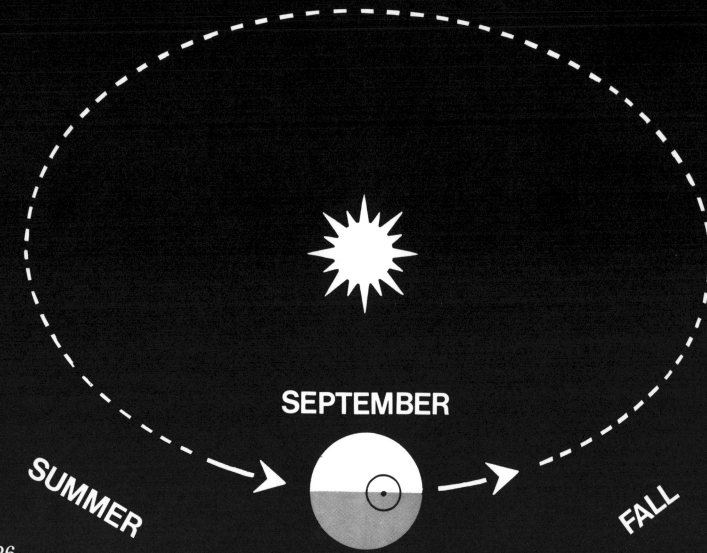

SEPTEMBER

SUMMER

FALL

Pumpkins are ripe.
Ducks and geese, robins
and many other birds
fly away to find a place
that's warmer. Soon it
will be winter.

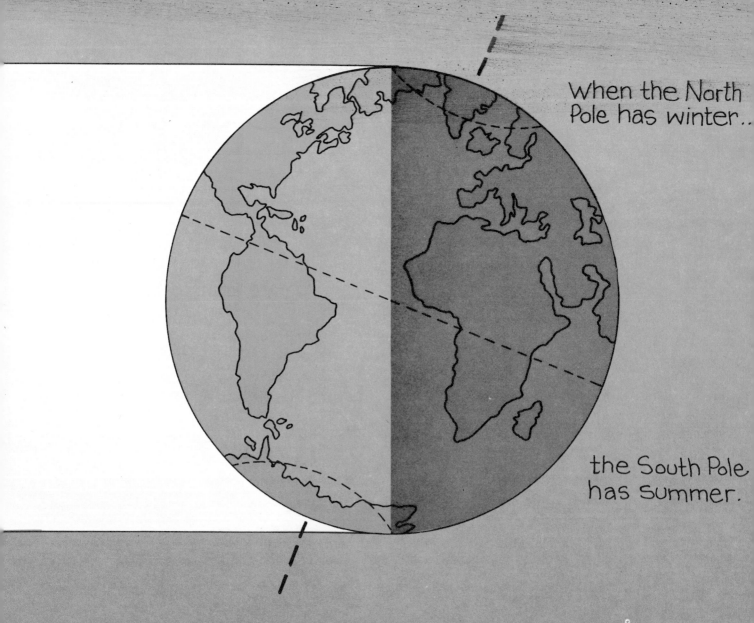

When the North Pole has winter...

the South Pole has summer.

In the southern part of the earth the weather gets warmer in the fall. Remember, seasons there are opposite to seasons in the north.

When your part of the earth has summer, another part has winter. When you have fall, other people have spring.

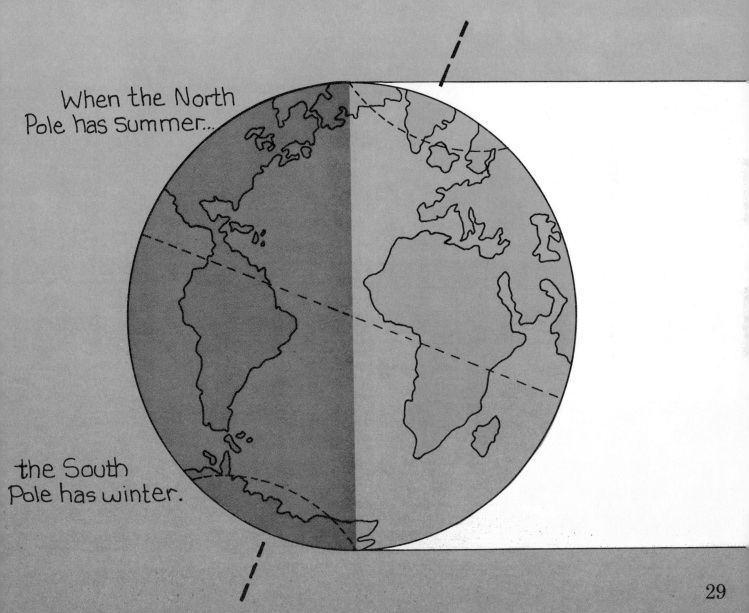

When the North Pole has summer...

the South Pole has winter.

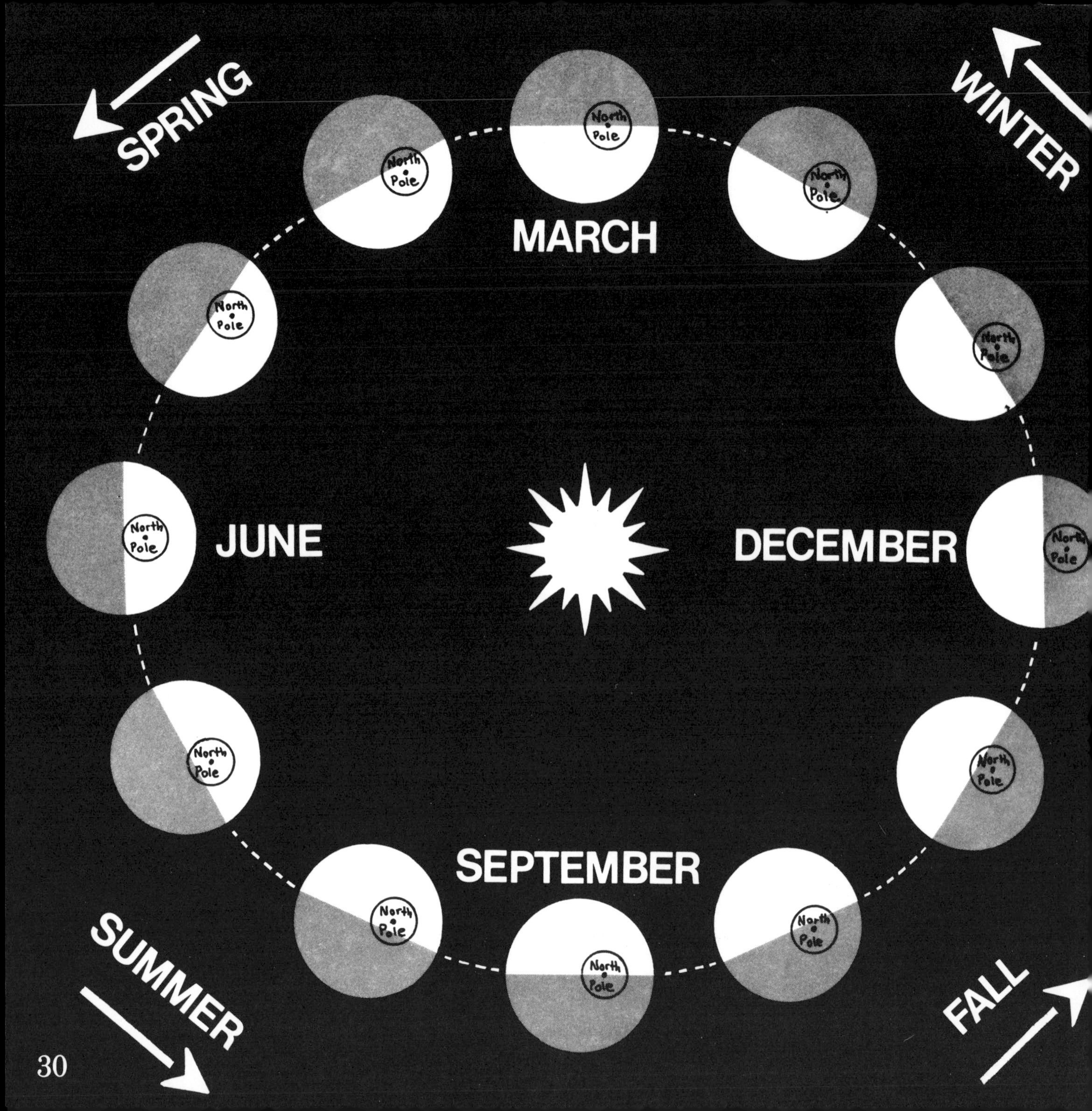

SPRING

MARCH

WINTER

JUNE

DECEMBER

SEPTEMBER

SUMMER

FALL

North Pole

30

SUMMER
FALL
WINTER
SPRING

Seasons change as a year goes by. They change
as earth revolves around the sun.

Seasons would not change if the axis of the
earth were straight up and down, and if the sun
did not warm the earth.

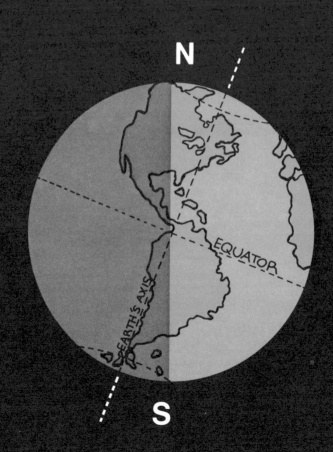

Sunshine makes the seasons—
sunshine and the
tilt of earth's axis.

ABOUT THE AUTHOR

Franklyn M. Branley, Astronomer Emeritus and former Chairman of The American Museum-Hayden Planetarium, is well known as the author of many books about astronomy and other sciences for young people of all ages. He is also coeditor of the Let's-Read-and-Find-Out Science Books.

Dr. Branley holds degrees from New York University, Columbia University, and the State University of New York College at New Paltz. He and his wife live in Woodcliff Lake, New Jersey.

ABOUT THE ILLUSTRATOR

When not involved with her primary love, illustration, Shelley Freshman enjoys sculpture, driving, astrology, nutrition, the theater, and playing the piano. Ms. Freshman was born in New York City and studied at the High School of Art and Design and at Pratt Institute. She is a member of the Society of Illustrators, and her work appears in the Illustrators' Annual Book.

Shelley Freshman lives in New York City with her Pisces dog, Jennie, but she says that between Jennie's barking and her own piano-playing they may be asked to move to Kentucky.